HIGH BRIDGE:
"THE END OF OUR
FIFTEEN MONTHS' LABOR"

In this large photograph, probably taken by Willis Vail, bridge workers are showing off their completed handiwork in early June 1914, about the same time that Vail wrote in his journal, "Thus we see the end of our 15 months' labor here."

High Bridge: "The End of Our Fifteen Months' Labor"

The story of building
the Norfolk & Western viaduct
near Farmville, Virginia

Illustrated with photographs by
Willis W. Vail
RESIDENT ENGINEER ON THE PROJECT

EDITED AND ANNOTATED BY
BOB FLIPPEN & RICHARD McCLINTOCK

FARMVILLE • 2014

Bob Flippen served as the AmeriCorps volunteer at High Bridge Trail State Park in 2011. After completing this mission, he joined the Park staff as an Education Specialist. He continues to develop interpretive programming and lead events designed to help visitors encounter history.

In 2011, Richard McClintock created an exhibit at the Virginia's Heartland Regional Visitor Center in downtown Farmville, Virginia. The exhibit, which explores the history and significance of High Bridge in its various forms, features a model of the 1853 bridge and many of the Vail photographs.

The editors express their thanks to WordwrightLLC.com for providing editorial and production assistance, and they gratefully acknowledge Rodney Vance of Farmville, Virginia, for his help in describing railroad techniques and technologies.

The Friends of High Bridge Trail State Park is a 501(c)(3) group of citizen volunteers. For more information or to purchase additional copies of this book, visit the group's website, *https://www.sites.google.com/site/friendsofhighbridgetrail,* or write Friends of High Bridge Trail State Park, 308B South Main Street #161, Farmville, VA 23901, or e-mail *fofhbt@gmail.com.* Proceeds from the sale of this book will support its programs to benefit the Park.

© 2014 Friends of High Bridge Trail State Park
All rights reserved. The Willis Vail photographs come from the collection of the Friends of High Bridge Trail State Park.
Printed in the United States of America.
ISBN 978-0-9960082-0-4

ON THE COVER: WILLIS W. VAIL, NEG. #1817 (1914), SHOWING THE NEW BRIDGE ON THE LEFT AND THE OLD ONE ON THE RIGHT (SEE PAGE 77).

HIGH BRIDGE:
"THE END OF OUR FIFTEEN MONTHS' LABOR"

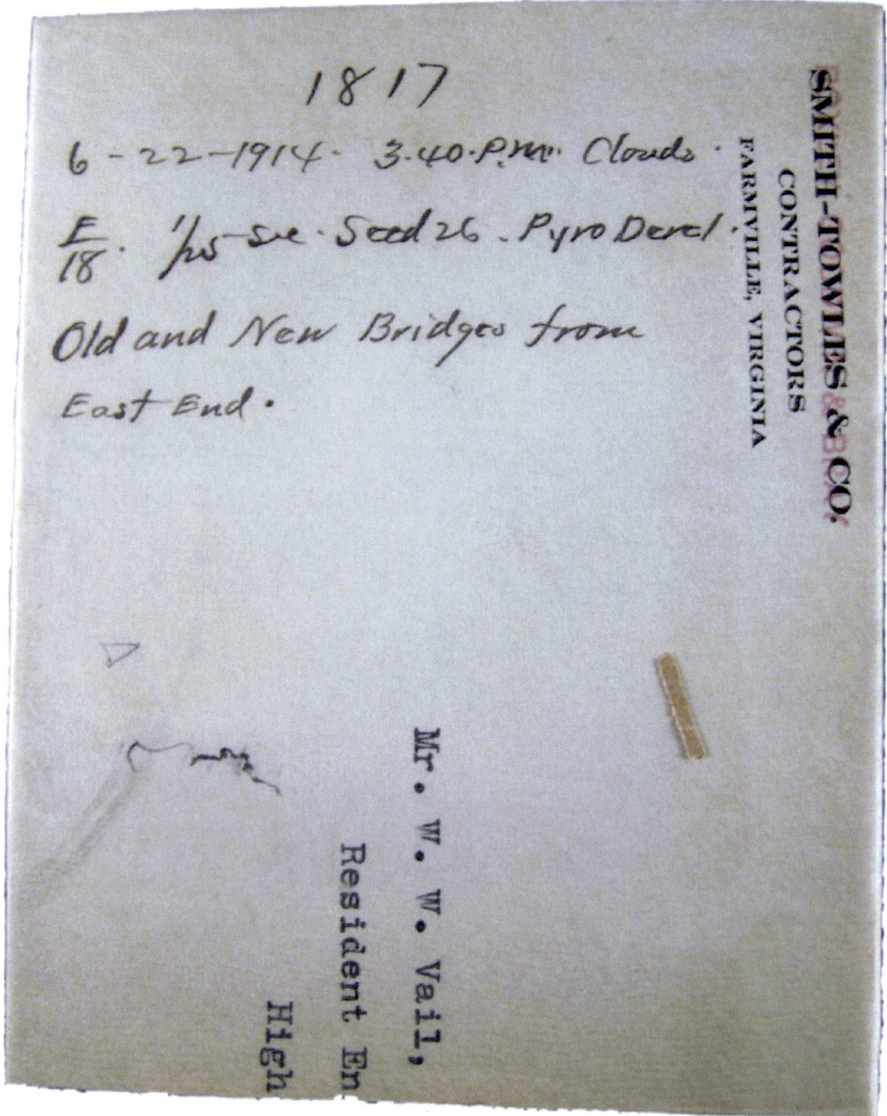

*Vail recycled envelopes to store his glass negatives.
This is an image of the envelope for Negative #1817 (for the photo on page 77).*

THE STORY OF A MARVELOUS FIND

In 2011, I was afforded a wonderful opportunity to serve High Bridge Trail State Park as an AmeriCorps volunteer. It was Virginia's newest State Park, a thirty-one-mile rails-to-trails conversion of an abandoned stretch of the Norfolk Southern Railway between Burkeville and Pamplin, with High Bridge serving as the anchor attraction. At the time, the bridge itself was undergoing rehabilitation that would eventually convert it for use by pedestrians, bicyclists, and equestrian traffic.

One of my tasks was to aid in the development and implementation of interpretive programming. Given a void of knowledge, interpreting the construction of the original 1853 High Bridge proved to be about as difficult as trying to describe how the Giza pyramids were built. As for the steel viaduct, a little more information was available. An article in the September 10, 1914, issue of *Engineering News,* accompanied with some grainy photographs, offered a glimpse into the process.

Then a marvel happened.

I received an e-mail from Eric Hougland, who was then Park Manager, asking me to investigate some photos of High Bridge he had discovered for sale. I was anticipating a series of reproduced photos taken by Timothy O'Sullivan in the summer of 1865. These popular reproductions are commonly traded.

Lo and behold, what I discovered were actual 4x5-inch glass negatives of photographs taken by Willis W. Vail, who served as the resident engineer on the 1913–14 construction project at High Bridge. The photos provided a treasure trove of details. I reported back that these artifacts, which were offered for sale by competitive bidding, were indeed significant. I recommended that the Park acquire them for its collection. I believed the visual images, combined with the written description in *Engineering News,* would provide material for interpretive programming and future exhibits.

Working through its affiliated Friends group, High Bridge Trail State Park was eventually able to acquire from the seller approximately half of the actual negatives and high-resolution scans of all the images.

In order to raise funds for the purchase, the Friends of High Bridge Trail State Park held a contest to award someone the privilege of being the first Park visitor to walk onto the newly rehabilitated High Bridge. Rodney Vance, of Farmville, Virginia, was the lucky winner. Together with his family, he strolled out onto the newly renovated bridge on April 4, 2012.

Now, for the first time, these historic images have been gathered together in book form. The pages that follow offer a fascinating photographic record detailing the people, equipment, and methods used to build the steel viaduct known as High Bridge during a fifteen-month construction period. It is with great pride that the Friends of High Bridge Trail State Park make this collection available for the public to enjoy.

Bob Flippen
Education Specialist
High Bridge Trail State Park

8 HIGH BRIDGE: "THE END OF OUR FIFTEEN MONTHS' LABOR"

Vail created this self-portrait of him at his desk in 1914. The image shows considerable technical skill in focusing on the brightly lit subject in the midst of the darkness.

WILLIS WILLSON VAIL, RESIDENT ENGINEER

Willis Willson Vail was born to John Vail and Mary Willson in Quakertown, New Jersey, on February 14, 1868. He attended Swarthmore College, near Philadelphia, and graduated in 1889 with a B.S. degree in Civil Engineering, specializing in surveying and railroad engineering. After graduation, he became an accomplished photographer and used this skill to document the progress of construction projects all over the United States.

From 1889 to 1894, Vail was employed as a surveyor for the Chesapeake & Ohio Railway and Norfolk & Western Railway. From 1897 to 1898, he worked with F.A. Dunham and F. J. Hubbard, Civil Engineers, on town surveys and other miscellaneous work. He was Assistant Engineer of the Central Railroad of New Jersey from 1899 to 1901 and became Chief Engineer of the Gulf and Ship Island Railroad in Gulfport, Mississippi, in 1905. Over the course of his life, he traveled through every state in the Union and extensively in Canada.

During a period spanning parts of 1913 and 1914, Vail was employed by the Norfolk & Western Railway as Resident Engineer near Farmville, Virginia, for the massive steel viaduct construction project known as High Bridge. For fifteen months he lived at the site and took photographs documenting the construction process and the people associated with it. Approximately 130 photographs were recorded on 4x5-inch glass negatives, and these views provide fascinating insight into construction practices of a century ago. Vail placed the negatives in protective sleeves he usually made from the corners of correspondence envelopes, trimmed to fit. On each was written a negative number (in a range between #1691 and #1827), the date, time, weather, lens aperture, and a brief description of the picture. The sleeves themselves often provide interesting details about the pictures.

These photos show Willis Vail as a student at Swarthmore College near Philadelphia.

While Vail worked in Virginia for the Norfolk & Western Railway, he met his future wife, Belle Gough of Lynchburg. They ultimately settled in New Jersey and made their residence in Quakertown in 1922, after purchasing the former home of John Lane.

Though he spent a good deal of his life away from Quakertown, Vail remained active in his hometown's affairs. He served as treasurer for Franklin Township (within which Quakertown was located), was a longtime member of the board of education, and founded the local Boy Scout Troop 108. During World War II, Vail corresponded with "his boys," men from Quakertown who served overseas. He also kept the local weather record for the United States Weather Bureau and maintained a large garden. Vail was a lifelong member of the Society of Friends and regularly attended its meetings in Buckingham, Pennsylvania. In addition to pursuing photography as a hobby, he was an avid stamp collector and amassed a large collection.

In 1947, on the occasion of his 79th birthday, more than 300 friends and family turned out to express their gratitude for all Vail had given to the community—and especially to its youth. A modest wooden school building which has been preserved in Quakertown bears a plaque in his honor. Vail died on August 4, 1951, at the age of 83. He was interred at the Locust Grove Cemetery in Quakertown, New Jersey.

In addition to the hundreds of people whose lives he enriched, Vail's legacy includes a valuable photographic record of early twentieth-century civil construction. Now that High Bridge Trail State Park has been able to acquire the images and glass negatives of the photographs that depict the steel viaduct's construction, his knowledge can be passed on to a new generation.

THE VAIL
HIGH BRIDGE
PHOTOGRAPH
COLLECTION

12 HIGH BRIDGE: "THE END OF OUR FIFTEEN MONTHS' LABOR"

This image depicts Norfolk & Western's passenger train No. 4 traversing the old High Bridge. The superstructure (the uppermost part of the bridge) first built in 1853, was replaced in 1870, 1886, and 1901. By 1912, the original brick piers were deteriorating, prompting construction of a new bridge. The railway in the foreground was temporary trackage used to transport materials to the new construction site. It branched off the mainline about a mile to the west, gradually working its way down into the Appomattox River floodplain.

HIGH BRIDGE: A VITAL LINK

The South Side Rail Road was chartered on March 5, 1846. Construction began in 1849 on a route developed to connect a series of County Courthouses between Petersburg and Lynchburg. The intended route across Prince Edward County passed through Prince Edward Courthouse (now Worsham), bypassing the town of Farmville entirely. To induce the rail line to come through town, prominent Farmville citizens pledged to purchase $100,000 in South Side Rail Road stock.

Although the initially proposed route never crossed the Appomattox River, the new route required traversing it twice. The longest crossing, a half-mile-wide river valley four miles east of Farmville, presented designers with a major construction challenge. Their solution was to build a massive viaduct.

A viaduct is a long bridge which carries a road of some sort (as opposed to an aqueduct, which carries water). The bridge rests on supporting pillars. In the case of the original High Bridge, these pillars were twenty brick piers. The structure's upper surface is called a deck, and it is held up from below by an architectural framework called a truss. Several trusses and the bracing between them form a span, which stretches from pillar to pillar. The original High Bridge construction featured twenty-one wooden spans, each made up of two parallel trusses. The earliest trusses were Howe trusses, a style that used only triangular bracing. In 1857, reinforcing arches were added, converting them to Burr arch trusses.

With construction complete, High Bridge became a vital link between Virginia's inland farm towns and the ocean shipping port of City Point on the James River. During the American Civil War, the bridge became even more strategic as armies relied on railroads to move troops and supplies swiftly. Nearing the war's end, as soldiers from the battered Confederate army retreated on April 7, 1865, they tried to burn High Bridge before Union forces could cross it. The attempt was only partially successful. Four western spans burned and collapsed, thereby rendering High Bridge impassable, but the wagon bridge below was captured intact. Federal forces used the wagon bridge to cross the river and continue their pursuit. Union engineers began building temporary spans to replace those that were destroyed. The railroad company later finished the work, and rail traffic resumed in September 1865.

As engines and loads became heavier, the High Bridge spans required upgrading or replacement. In 1870, a type of iron truss known as a Fink truss replaced the original wooden superstructure. Renovations in 1886 with a Pratt deck truss, another type of iron construction that featured a lighter and stronger design, helped to further reinforce the structure.

By the turn of the century, heavier trains required additional supports. In 1901, a fourth superstructure, which added a third truss to reinforce the existing trusses, was constructed along with a metal floor system. At the same time, railway engineers reinforced the old brick piers with angle-iron corner braces to prevent them from collapsing.

Finally, in 1912, the Norfolk & Western Railway decided to build a new structure alongside the original. Plans called for a new bridge that would rest on steel towers instead of brick piers and that would stand seven feet taller than the original structure.

14 HIGH BRIDGE: "THE END OF OUR FIFTEEN MONTHS' LABOR"

This picture is the first photo taken by Vail as the project began in 1913. It looks eastward across the old High Bridge deck.

HIGH BRIDGE: "THE END OF OUR FIFTEEN MONTHS' LABOR" 15

This view of the old bridge from its west end shows the Pratt deck trusses (installed in 1886) on the original brick piers (built in 1853). Steel bands and angle-iron corner braces helped strengthen the weakening piers. Wooden poles (seen at the far right) made a protective casing around the brick abutment that supported the end of the bridge.

Norfolk & Western Railway engineers worked in an office on the construction site. Most of the engineers were young men—Vail called them "the boys." This image, taken in 1913, shows the men looking over the High Bridge plans.

PLANS AND PLANNERS

The Norfolk & Western Railway maintained its own engineering department, which was responsible for projects along its entire line. When railroad officials made the decision to replace High Bridge, the bridge designers who worked for the company swung into action. Their tasks included analyzing the weight of traffic the new bridge would have to bear and the most efficient way to build a structure to support it.

When planning work began, Charles S. Churchill served as Chief Engineer for Norfolk & Western, and J. E. Crawford held the title of Bridge Engineer. Crawford's duties included preparing the masonry plans and supervising the design of the steelwork. Crawford later succeeded Churchill as Chief Engineer, and the 1913–14 work at High Bridge was completed under Crawford's supervision.

The engineer with day-to-day responsibility at the construction site was Willis W. Vail. Because he lived on site, he held the title Resident Engineer. His duties included reviewing the plans prepared by the N&W engineering department, coordinating the stages of construction, and making plans for incidental projects like construction trackage and borrow pits.

Several companies assisted in the project. Cummings Structural Concrete Co., of Pittsburgh, Pennsylvania, manufactured the concrete piles. The Virginia Bridge & Iron Co., of Roanoke, Virginia, designed and furnished the steelwork and then erected the structure. Contractors W. W. Boxley & Co., also of Roanoke, built the masonry abutments and approaches. Abutments are the structures that support the ends of the bridge, and the approaches are the pathways that lead to the bridge while maintaining the required grade.

In order to accommodate eastbound coal traffic, the bridge had to stay within guidelines that permitted changes in elevation no more than sixteen feet per mile (a 0.3% grade). Achieving this necessitated the construction of an approach of 1,800′ in length at the bridge's western end and one of 400′ at the eastern end.

The new approaches were to be built up using fill dirt from nearby excavations called borrow pits. Because local soils contained large quantities of talc and soapstone, they were prone to slipping. To address this issue, project planners designed approaches that would be built in layers with the bottoms much wider than the tops.

The new bridge's design utilized forty-three spans and twenty-one towers. The end spans, called abutment spans, were each 90′ long. Short spans that crossed the tops of the towers, called tower spans, were 38′ long. Spans between the towers, called intermediate spans, were 72′ long. All the towers were constructed of steel, and each would stand on four massive concrete pedestals fabricated on the site.

Building the bridge took fifteen months, from April 1913 through June 1914. Dismantling the old bridge took another five weeks.

18 HIGH BRIDGE: "THE END OF OUR FIFTEEN MONTHS' LABOR"

A tar-papered building, situated on the north side of the construction site, housed the office used by the engineers who were working on location.

HIGH BRIDGE: "THE END OF OUR FIFTEEN MONTHS' LABOR" 19

This photograph, taken from the old bridge, shows the workers' camp beside the temporary construction railway. The building used as an office for the engineers appears near the middle, just above and to the right of center. The residence and barn in the distance belonged to Cary Smith.

20 HIGH BRIDGE: "THE END OF OUR FIFTEEN MONTHS' LABOR"

Angle-iron corner braces connected by iron rods supported the deteriorating brick piers of the old bridge. This image depicts the condition of these structures as work began at the site.

PREPARING THE SITE

Before any actual construction could take place, the site had to be surveyed, graded, and made accessible to the heavy equipment that would be used to build the bridge.

After the surveyors did their work, the next step was to build a temporary railway system that could be used to deliver materials and machinery to the base of operations in the valley, far below the existing mainline track. Although the temporary track could have a much steeper grade than the mainline track, it still had to stay within acceptable limits. This meant that it had to branch off the mainline and begin its descent more than a mile west of the bridge.

Different types of temporary railways were involved. One was a standard-gauge branch. In a standard-gauge track, the rails are 4′8½″ apart. The standard-gauge line was used to bring freight cars down from the mainline and to carry cranes with huge clamshell buckets that were used to dig holes for the foundations. A narrow-gauge line designed for lighter equipment and with rails that were closer together was used for carrying specialty cars, such as those which transported fresh concrete in removable vats. A dual-gauge track offering both standard-gauge and narrow-gauge options was constructed by adding a third rail within the standard-gauge tracks so that the two systems shared one rail in common.

Workers also had to assemble other temporary structures to support the construction project. One type of structure that had multiple uses was called a trestle. Although many people think of a trestle as a special kind of bridge, in a more generic way the term refers to a kind of frame in which a horizontal crosspiece (called a stringer) is supported with spindly legs (which are called bents). During the work at High Bridge, some trestles were built and then the bents were buried with fill dirt. This created dirt-fill structures that were able to withstand more weight than the trestle alone. Wooden trestles used in this way were eventually buried at both ends of High Bridge where the abutments uphold the ends of the bridge.

Trestles were also used as structures within temporary rail systems constructed to help move fill dirt across the construction site. After their purpose had been fulfilled, such temporary trestles were torn down or relocated. They were not buried in dirt like other trestles.

Work began by clearing brush and dumping the first loads of fill for the new abutments, the foundational structures that would support the ends of the new bridge.

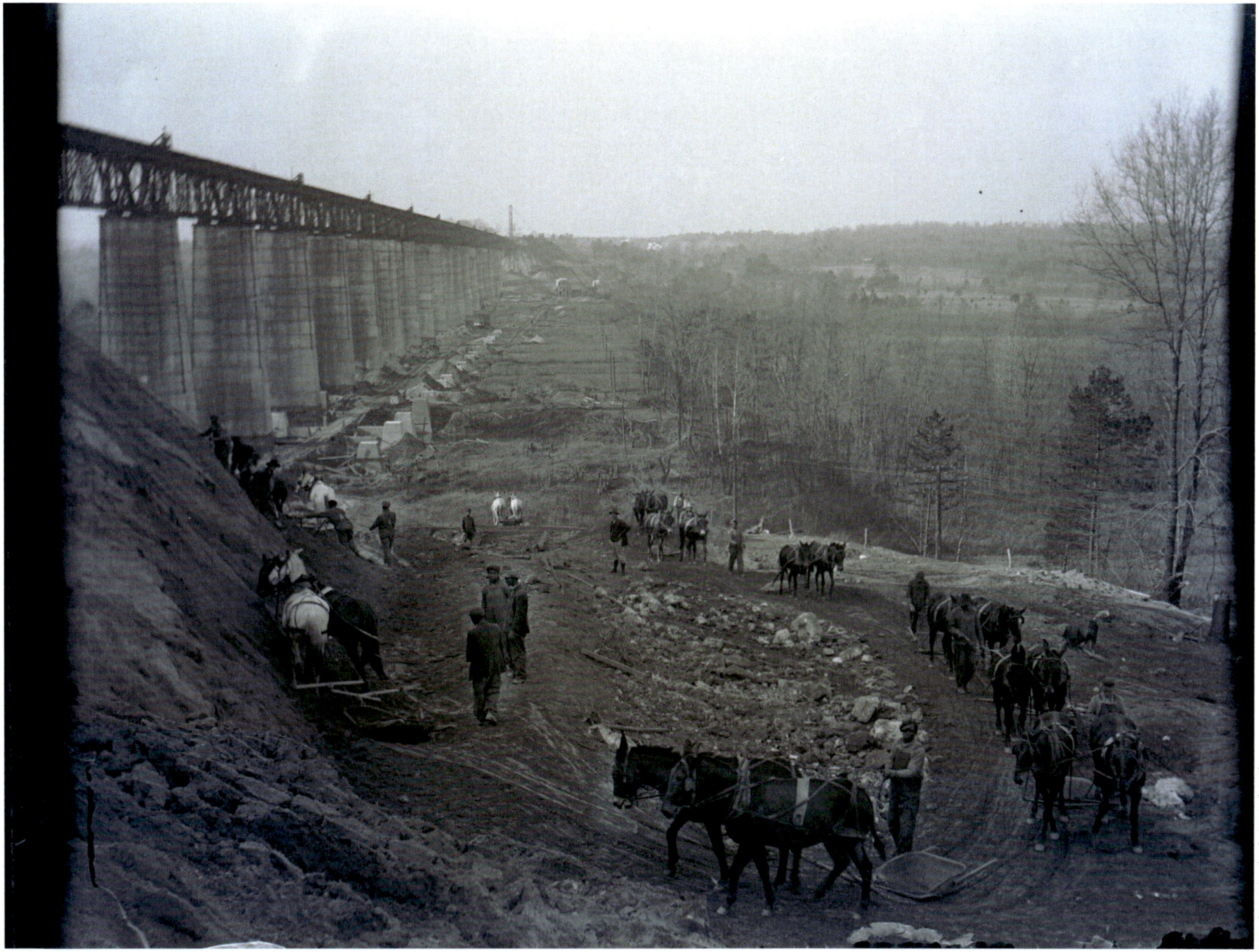

WILLIS W. VAIL, NEG. #1766 (1913)

Local farmers with teams of horses and mules pulled scoops and graders. Scoops were used to haul fill dirt, and graders helped to smooth the terrain.

Dirt used as fill was deposited on the downstream side of the bridge. Teams of horses carried it from there to the other side and spread it as needed.

HIGH BRIDGE: "THE END OF OUR FIFTEEN MONTHS' LABOR" 25

After clearing away trees and grading the site of the new bridge, workers built an access railway, a water tower, and a concrete plant. This image depicts these structures and a miniature locomotive, known as a donkey. The donkey was used on the temporary narrow-gauge railway to trundle vats of concrete to the pedestal bases.

26 HIGH BRIDGE: "THE END OF OUR FIFTEEN MONTHS' LABOR"

Supplies traveled to the construction site via a temporary standard-gauge access railway. To reach the construction site on the valley's floor, its grade had to be substantially steeper than that of the mainline railway.

Steam shovels, like those used to build the Panama Canal, excavated mountains of soil to be used as fill in creating the new approaches.

POWERFUL TOOLS

Workers relied on hand labor when building the first High Bridge in 1853. By the time the steel bridge was constructed in 1913–14, powerful steam equipment and other heavy-duty gear could be put to use. Although these tools represented a major improvement over hand labor, they do not match the power of equipment used today.

Tons of gravel were shipped in from quarries all along the railroad's mainline. This photograph shows a clamshell bucket at work.

Caissons are box-like structures with walls that hold back the soil around an excavated area. At High Bridge they were used in constructing the foundations for tower pedestals. This image shows a crane driving in the interlocking steel panels that formed the side of a caisson.

Workers built wooden frames inside the metal caissons and then filled the frames with concrete. This image depicts an orange-peel bucket being used inside a caisson during the construction of a tower pedestal's foundation.

HIGH BRIDGE: "THE END OF OUR FIFTEEN MONTHS' LABOR" 31

Steam-powered locomotive cranes lifted heavy equipment and moved concrete. The crane shown in this image was built of wood. Other cranes were made of metal (see the next photo).

32 HIGH BRIDGE: "THE END OF OUR FIFTEEN MONTHS' LABOR"

Work continued year-round, even in the snow. This metal crane sits astride the dual-gauge track, which used three rails to create a standard-gauge line and a narrow-gauge track within it.

This view of the Western Spreader Car shows both wings at work. "Western Spreader" was the manufacturer's name for the equipment. The doubled rail at left was designed to keep the cars from derailing on the irregular temporary track.

A rail-mounted spreader with retractable wings smoothed fresh applications of fill dirt. In this image the markings of the construction firm Boxley, Goodwin, & Bray can be seen on the spreader.

In this image, Norfolk & Western's passenger train No. 7 is crossing the old bridge. The layered dirt structure shows the stages required to elevate the new approach. The triangular structure near the front of the train is a pile driver that was used to pound long steel-reinforced concrete piles into the fill dirt to support the new bridge's abutments.

FILLS AND FOUNDATIONS

Because the new bridge stood seven feet higher than the old bridge and off to its side, it was necessary to construct long structures called approaches at both ends of the bridge. The approaches were built using fill dirt that was excavated with a steam shovel from nearby borrow pits—areas where soil (or another material, such as gravel) is excavated for use in another location. The soil obtained from the borrow pits near High Bridge contained talc and soapstone, a combination that made it susceptible to slippage and increased the risk for landslides.

Because of this risk, several structural precautions had to be taken. The borrow pits themselves required careful engineering guidance. Vail's journal recounts an episode where he spent an entire day working on cross-sectional plans for them. In addition, the design of the approaches called for structures that would be twice as wide as they were high, a strategy intended to help minimize dangers related to slips.

Engineers also had to keep a careful eye on the slope at the edge of the fill. Even when gradients were carefully controlled, heavy rains could cause landslides. The approaches were constructed in three separate tiers, called lifts. A ditch around the base helped provide drainage. The approach at the west end of the bridge is about 1,800′ long, and the one at the east end is 400′ long. Combined, they used 471,000 cubic yards of fill dirt.

Workers built the approaches using a process that employed wooden trestles and fill dirt. Surveyors marked the dimensions of the area to be filled, and then workmen built a wooden trestle where the fill dirt was to go. Engines shunted special cars with tipping compartments out onto the trestle to dump dirt over the side. As the fill rose, the trestles gradually disappeared inside the growing mounds of dirt. Presumably the trestles are there still.

A total of eighty-four concrete pedestals were constructed to support the new bridge's steel towers. Each pedestal was individually identified by a number, beginning at the eastern end. The pedestals were roughly pyramidal in shape, with flat square tops. They each had the same width dimensions, but they differed in height. Pedestals at the ends of the bridge were twenty to forty feet high, and next to the river they were twenty feet high. Elsewhere along the bridge in the middle, pedestals measured eight feet high. Much of the height of the pedestals was buried under fill.

HIGH BRIDGE: "THE END OF OUR FIFTEEN MONTHS' LABOR" 37

Workers built several temporary trestles over the locations where fill was to be added. In order to maintain a safe slope on the approach, the fill's base had to be far wider than its eventual width at the top, where the mainline track would be laid. Here one of the temporary wooden trestles is seen from below.

38   HIGH BRIDGE: "THE END OF OUR FIFTEEN MONTHS' LABOR"

This picture, taken from a vantage point on the old bridge, shows a pair of temporary trestles and the fill train in action. The last car is the spreader, ready to grade what the cars ahead of it have deposited. The concrete plant sits in the foreground. Its former service tracks are being covered by the fill.

HIGH BRIDGE: "THE END OF OUR FIFTEEN MONTHS' LABOR" 39

Trains of hydraulic dump cars were driven out onto the trestles, where the fill dirt was dumped, gradually burying the trestles.

40   HIGH BRIDGE: "THE END OF OUR FIFTEEN MONTHS' LABOR"

Landslides were a constant threat with newly poured fill. The Engineering News *article states that the soil near the construction site contained talc and soapstone, which amplified its tendency to slip. This image depicts a landslide that occurred in December 1913.*

As trestles were covered with fill, they were abandoned, and new temporary tracks were laid to transport more fill.

MAKING CONCRETE

A plant at the worksite provided the concrete needed. Workers dredged sand from the Appomattox River using a barge they built and called "Titanic." A steam engine installed on the barge both propelled it and pumped sand from the riverbed. At the concrete plant, cement and coarse aggregate (crushed limestone) were added to the sand. Special vat cars on the narrow-gauge construction railway then carried the wet concrete to where workers needed it.

The onsite concrete plant sat on the floodplain at the west end of the bridge. Sand from the dredge had to travel the length of the construction track to supply the mixer. This image features the concrete plant in the foreground with complex layers of track that covered one another as work progressed.

HIGH BRIDGE: "THE END OF OUR FIFTEEN MONTHS' LABOR" 43

Vail photographed these workers as they built a barge to dredge sand from the Appomattox River for the onsite concrete plant.

44 HIGH BRIDGE: "THE END OF OUR FIFTEEN MONTHS' LABOR"

The barge's builders called it "Titanic" in honor of the disaster from a year earlier, which was apparently still fresh in their minds.

HIGH BRIDGE: "THE END OF OUR FIFTEEN MONTHS' LABOR" 45

This image depicts the "Titanic" at work, dredging sand upstream from the old bridge. Some concrete pedestals for the new bridge can be seen at the bottom right.

46   HIGH BRIDGE: "THE END OF OUR FIFTEEN MONTHS' LABOR"

Here workers can be seen unloading sand from the "Titanic." The center of the barge's hull was filled with wet sand from the riverbed.

HIGH BRIDGE: "THE END OF OUR FIFTEEN MONTHS' LABOR" 47

Workmen used a steam crane to load river sand into the mixer. A narrow-gauge donkey locomotive pulled special vat cars which were filled with fresh concrete. The donkey's cab can be seen in this image in the foreground, at the left.

Bags of cement arrived on freight cars via the standard-gauge line. They were then loaded onto a cart and pulled by the hoisting engine's cables (see the next image) up a steep ramp to the mixer.

HIGH BRIDGE: "THE END OF OUR FIFTEEN MONTHS' LABOR" 49

The hoisting engine was a steam-driven winch. The cylindrical object is the vertical boiler of the steam engine. The cables are pulling a concrete cart like the one on the previous image.

50 HIGH BRIDGE: "THE END OF OUR FIFTEEN MONTHS' LABOR"

The concrete plant had its own tramway for hauling concrete up to the west abutment. In this picture, one of the temporary fill trestles is to the right of the abutment.

HIGH BRIDGE: "THE END OF OUR FIFTEEN MONTHS' LABOR" 51

This image shows the donkey engine backing its train to the crane, which is lifting a vat of fresh concrete to dump into the wooden form for Pedestal 3, at the east end of the bridge. The three rails of the dual-gauge tracks can be seen in the foreground. The donkey engine is on the narrow-gauge rails; the crane is on the standard-gauge track.

ABUTMENTS AND PILE DRIVING

The abutments were U-shaped masonry structures that supported the end spans of the bridge. Each abutment included a main wall and two wing walls. All the walls employed steel-rail reinforcement, and the space between the wing walls was filled with broken stone and earth.

Because the abutments served the purpose of transferring the load from the bridge's structure to its foundation, they required secure footings that reached through the fresh fill to solid rock. To meet this need, workers constructed massive 40′ to 60′ steel-reinforced concrete piles.

To make the piles, workers used reinforcing rods tied together with wire. First, they would weave a steel skeleton of the required length. Then they put that framework into a huge mold and poured concrete around it. Each pile had to cure for thirty to sixty days before it could be driven into the ground.

Workers used a crane to lift cured piles into position on the pile driver. The pile driver employed a 12,000-pound hammer which dropped repeatedly, forcing a pile into the earth until only the top foot or so remained above ground. Work progressed at a rate of about ¾″ per blow, and each pile took about half a day to drive into place.

Pile-driving was dangerous work, especially when the top of a pile would crack under the pressure and spray shards in all directions. When a pile was broken, it was cut off and another was driven beside it. After the piles were driven into place, workers cast a concrete foundation for the abutment on top of them.

Only a small number of piles were damaged.
This picture shows a shattered pile.

HIGH BRIDGE: "THE END OF OUR FIFTEEN MONTHS' LABOR" 53

Workers built a skeleton of reinforcing rods for each pile.

After laying the steel skeleton in a mold, workers poured concrete around it to form the pile's octagonal profile. The wooden forms were removed after two days, and each pile was allowed to cure for thirty to sixty days before driving. This worker is smoothing concrete in a mold freshly filled by other workers using large-wheeled barrows. A temporary fill trestle can be seen in the background.

HIGH BRIDGE: "THE END OF OUR FIFTEEN MONTHS' LABOR" 55

Lifting piles into position on the driver (above, at the bridge's west end) was a delicate operation, because any twist or jolt could fracture the concrete.

The work of driving piles went on even in the snow (above, at the east end of the bridge).

56 HIGH BRIDGE: "THE END OF OUR FIFTEEN MONTHS' LABOR"

Like most of the machines used on the bridge, the pile driver was powered by a steam engine with a vertical boiler. The image to the left shows the boiler beside the hammer framework at the west end of the bridge. The image at the right shows the equipment at the east end.

Piles for the abutments had to be long enough to penetrate through the fill to the original ground line. Here piles have been driven into the fill to support the east abutment.

58 HIGH BRIDGE: "THE END OF OUR FIFTEEN MONTHS' LABOR"

This image illustrates piles in place for the west abutment base. A wooden form for casting concrete surrounds them.

PIERS AND PEDESTALS

The spans of the old High Bridge, constructed in 1853, were supported by brick piers. Bricks were chosen for two reasons. They could support more weight than wood, and bricks were estimated to be considerably less costly than stone because a superior quality of clay from which to make them was available nearby. Iron rods passing through the brick piers anchored the original wooden superstructure to the foundation.

As time went on, vibration from heavy trains traveling across the bridge caused some of the brick piers to crack. To strengthen the structures, Norfolk & Western installed angle-iron corner braces connected by iron rods at intervals of about eight feet. The continued appearance of additional cracks in the piers, along with an anticipated increase in rail traffic, led to the decision to build the new steel viaduct.

Work on the new bridge was planned so that it could move forward without endangering the piers for the old bridge, which was still in use during the construction phase. The old piers can be seen in many of the images depicting the erection of the new bridge.

Instead of piers, the new bridge featured a type of construction that employed steel towers resting on concrete pedestals. There were twenty-one towers along the length of the bridge. Each tower had four legs, and each leg stood on a concrete pedestal. The pedestals were 6′ square on top and 8′8″ square at the base. Each pedestal was placed on a 12′8″ square foundation that itself sat on bedrock. The pedestals were capable of carrying a load of 7.3 tons per square foot.

Most of the pedestals along the length of the bridge were 8′ high; however, the pedestals supporting the first towers from either end of the bridge and those adjacent to the river were taller. They varied from 20′ to 40′ high, but much of their height was eventually covered with fill.

To build the pedestals, workers first dug large holes using steam cranes with clamshell or orange-peel scoops. In the holes, they built square steel-walled caissons, 16′ on each side and 20′ or more deep. Next, carpenters built wooden molds in the shape of the pedestal. Inside those forms, steelworkers erected meshes of reinforcing rods. Concrete was made in the onsite plant. Cranes with long booms were used to lift huge vats of fresh concrete off the narrow-gauge cars on the work track and pour the concrete into the molds.

After the concrete cured, the top surface of the pedestals needed to be planed to make an exactly level base for the legs of the tower. This precise task was done by hand with hammers and chisels.

This image depicts a crane positioning a concrete vat over the form for a pedestal foundation. The undercarriage of the narrow-gauge car, which had been used to transport the concrete vat, can be seen between the engine and the crane.

After the donkey engine brought concrete from the plant, a crane carried the vat to the form, where workers emptied its contents.

62 HIGH BRIDGE: "THE END OF OUR FIFTEEN MONTHS' LABOR"

The pedestals shown in this picture stand near the west abutment. In the foreground on the right, a workhorse can be seen pulling materials into place. High in the background, fill dirt (poured out by the hydraulic dump cars) tumbles down a hill beside a trestle.

WILLIS W. VAIL, NEG. #1752 (1913)

HIGH BRIDGE: "THE END OF OUR FIFTEEN MONTHS' LABOR" 63

Pedestals supporting the towers at each end of the bridge were between 20' and 40' high. They were taller than other pedestals, and their lower parts were later covered by fill. The height of a worker standing beside the pedestal base demonstrates the massive size of these pedestals.

64 HIGH BRIDGE: "THE END OF OUR FIFTEEN MONTHS' LABOR"

After each pedestal was cast and cured, its top surface needed to be leveled for placement of the steel beams. In this image Henry Howell, a master craftsman, chips away at the concrete to level it.

HIGH BRIDGE: "THE END OF OUR FIFTEEN MONTHS' LABOR" 65

Workmen with the responsibility of ensuring that the pedestals were straight and level were called planers or dressers. The three men working on the pedestal top in this image have not been identified.

66 HIGH BRIDGE: "THE END OF OUR FIFTEEN MONTHS' LABOR"

The dual-gauge construction track had its own low-lying bridge across the Appomattox River. It was almost overwhelmed when the river swelled during a heavy winter rain. The footings for the new bridge can be seen interwoven among the old piers. This tactic was used so that the construction project could proceed without interrupting train traffic on the old bridge.

FROM WILLIS VAIL'S JOURNAL:
*January 4, 1914 - Rained night before last and most of yesterday. The river is up to the top of its banks and running a little over the bottom.
January 5, 1914 - The River reached its highest about midnight last night, but did not get up on Towle's [the contractor's] track.*

HIGH BRIDGE: "THE END OF OUR FIFTEEN MONTHS' LABOR" 67

Setting the steelwork began by bolting the lower parts of the towers to their pedestals and assembling them as high as the cranes on the ground could reach. Cranes at the bridge level then took over, lifting prefabricated top sections into position. The track on the new bridge was laid as the process moved forward. This picture features two cranes at work, one below (lower right) and one above (upper left).

STEELWORK

The steel components of the bridge included its spans and towers. Each tower consisted of two structures called bents (essentially the framework that comprised the tower legs) and cross lattices that provided support and strength. Spans were formed from two long steel girders connected by steel cross-bracing. Workers constructed the ties and track on top of the spans after the spans were installed on the towers.

Virginia Bridge & Iron Company of Roanoke manufactured the steel girders and spans for the new bridge. Their workers then came to Farmville to install the steelwork. As each tower was completed using a crane at the track level, ties and rails were set, and the crane moved forward to work on the next tower.

Because most of the pieces had been prepared beforehand, the steelwork assembly went very quickly. Erection of the steel began on April 1, 1914. The first girder was set in place two days later. The last span was set on June 3. Workmen completed the final touches—the cross bracing between girders and riveting—on June 11. The floor and the track upon it were finished on June 18, and the new bridge carried its first train on June 22, 1914.

The process of setting the steelwork began at the east end. This image shows assembled sections of the towers ready to be lifted into place. An article in Engineering News *(September 1914) boasted that the new High Bridge contained 6,995,628 pounds of metal.*

HIGH BRIDGE: "THE END OF OUR FIFTEEN MONTHS' LABOR" 69

Vail must have been particularly excited about setting the first girder. This image begins a series of closely timed photographs that document the process. This photograph shows the girder resting on the lip of the east abutment, ready to be lifted into place.

In this image, the crane has picked up the girder and is swinging it around to be parallel to the bridge. For the 90' spans next to the abutments, individual girders were laid and later braced and riveted. The 38' tower spans and 72' intermediate spans were assembled before installation.

HIGH BRIDGE: "THE END OF OUR FIFTEEN MONTHS' LABOR" 71

Here the first girder for the abutment span is being guided down into place. One of the workers can be seen standing on a tower and another rides on the beam itself. Each girder was 7½' high.

72   HIGH BRIDGE: "THE END OF OUR FIFTEEN MONTHS' LABOR"

This image, taken from the west abutment, illustrates the process of erecting the steelwork. All the tower bases have been placed and work is proceeding on upper sections of the towers.

A crane with an 80' boom rode the rails on the newly placed spans. First it lifted the upper part of the next tower section into place; then it positioned the next span. After track was laid, it moved forward and repeated the process. Tower and intermediate spans were prefabricated as complete units.

Vail labeled this photograph, "Setting span 42, taken from camp." Spans on top of the towers, like this one being lowered into place, were much shorter than spans between towers.

HIGH BRIDGE: "THE END OF OUR FIFTEEN MONTHS' LABOR" 75

As was the case with the eastern abutment span, the western abutment span was built by setting individual girders that were later braced and riveted. This image and the next depict the setting of the last girder at the bridge's western end.

76 HIGH BRIDGE: "THE END OF OUR FIFTEEN MONTHS' LABOR"

The inscription "To Columbus" that can be seen on the last girder as it is lowered into place indicates that it was the western end. Below it a workman can be seen standing on the old bridge, which was seven feet lower than the new one. He appears as a tiny, distant onlooker. On May 27, Vail wrote in his journal, "One of the girders of the last span was set today, and after the men quit work I walked across the new bridge."

WILLIS W. VAIL, NEG. #1815 (1914)

HIGH BRIDGE: "THE END OF OUR FIFTEEN MONTHS' LABOR" 77

When ties and rail had been laid on the new bridge, Vail took this portrait of the old and new bridges together. This view was not long available. The old bridge was gone within weeks after the new one was completed. Modern worker-safety regulations would not have approved the sagging boards that workmen used to cross from one bridge to the other.

AWAY WITH THE OLD

Demolition of the old bridge began on July 1, 1914, two weeks after rail traffic switched to the new bridge. A steam crane rode over from the eastern end, lifted the westernmost trusses one by one, and carried them back to a deposit area near Rice, where workers dismantled them for recycling. Working backward, span by span, the process continued until August 12, 1914, when the old bridge's superstructure was gone. The brick piers and old abutments were left in place, except for the pier in the Appomattox River (at right in the image on page 66), which was demolished at the request of government engineers who feared that it would inhibit navigation on the river.

During World War II, when resources were scarce, bricks from the westernmost six and a half piers found new lives in nearby building projects. These included a factory addition in Farmville, a schoolhouse in Prospect, and numerous homes. Today, the old abutments and twelve and a half of the original brick piers remain as a mute testimony to the original High Bridge's years of history and service to the railroad.

A crane removes the first truss from the old bridge as an engineer looks on. The workmen near the center of the picture are standing on the supplementary truss which was installed in 1901 between the 1886 trusses.

HIGH BRIDGE: "THE END OF OUR FIFTEEN MONTHS' LABOR" 79

After carrying the truss across the bridge, the crane deposited it at the scrapping yard near Rice.

80 HIGH BRIDGE: "THE END OF OUR FIFTEEN MONTHS' LABOR"

The crane then laid the truss on its side so workmen could more easily reach it for disassembly.

In the last stage of the process, workers disassembled the old trusses for recycling as scrap iron.

THE MEN WHO BUILT THE BRIDGE

It is unknown exactly how many men worked on the 1914 steel bridge, but they probably numbered several hundred. They were exposed to dangers and conditions that modern workers might eschew. They walked on single beams high in the air and rode iron girders as they swung from a locomotive crane. They lived at the site in a makeshift village of huts covered with tar paper. Some came from the local area and others from far away, often riding the railroad home to their families on the weekends.

The nearby town of Farmville was a popular place to visit. Workers traveled there for supplies and entertaining diversions like The Chautauqua, a traveling show featuring people with various musical talents and educational lectures.

T. W. Brooks III of Jacksonville, Florida, the grandson of one of the bridge contractors, recalls this tale: "Daddy told me that when T. W. [Brooks] Sr. [seen in the center of the photograph below] was building the bridge, the workers were concerned about getting paid. To quell the fears of the workers, he bought two supposedly equal diamonds. One was made into a man's ring and the other was a diamond stickpin. He had an agreement with a Farmville bank that if the payroll did not come through on payday, the bank would advance the payroll using the diamonds as collateral. The men were aware of the agreement with the bank and T. W. Sr. openly wore the diamonds, so the workers didn't worry about getting paid. Daddy told me a story about the day someone noticed that the stickpin was gone. He said that all of the workers gathered around and the steam shovel moved the dirt back and forth with all eyes watching and trying to spot the diamond. After more than six hours of this exercise, someone spotted the twinkle and the stickpin was found. It turns out that the diamonds were not exactly the same. One was 1.48 carats and the other was 1.53 carats."

Vail took this picture of J. W. Goodwin, T. W. Brooks, Sr., and G. Gibboney standing on the porch of the Commissary (or general store) which served the work force.

HIGH BRIDGE: "THE END OF OUR FIFTEEN MONTHS' LABOR"   83

Although the names of most of the bridge workmen are unknown, Vail's notes identify this man as Henry Howell, a master craftsman who worked with concrete (see page 64).

Uncle John (Winfield) Redd, a night watchman, has also been identified. Vail took this photograph of him standing on the old bridge. Redd's descendants still live in the nearby area.

84 HIGH BRIDGE: "THE END OF OUR FIFTEEN MONTHS' LABOR"

Workmen building the new High Bridge did dangerous work, apparently undeterred by the risks, judging by the casual way they stood on the edge of the old bridge or handled the sixty-foot pile about to be driven into the fill dirt to support the eastern abutment.

HIGH BRIDGE: "THE END OF OUR FIFTEEN MONTHS' LABOR" 85

Today nothing remains of this camp where bridge workers lived except a cast-iron pump-head from the well that provided the camp's fresh water supply.

86 HIGH BRIDGE: "THE END OF OUR FIFTEEN MONTHS' LABOR"

Vail notes that he took this picture of unidentified workers in front of one of the dormitory buildings at the camp on Sunday, January 25, 1914. His remark on the image sleeve mentions that the camera was out of focus.

HIGH BRIDGE: "THE END OF OUR FIFTEEN MONTHS' LABOR" 87

Vail and his fellow engineers apparently took full advantage of the Appomattox River. This photograph, taken sometime during the last days on the job, shows J. A. Jamison diving into the river.

88 HIGH BRIDGE: "THE END OF OUR FIFTEEN MONTHS' LABOR"

Vail writes in his journal that on one sunny day he and "the boys" went swimming. This image suggests they were confident that no one was looking.

APPENDICES

Engineering News

VOLUME 72   SEPTEMBER 10, 1914   NUMBER 11

The Farmville High Bridge across the Appomattox Valley

BY F. P. TURNER*

One of the longest and highest bridges on the Norfolk & Western Ry., known as Farmville High Bridge, has just been rebuilt as a double-track structure in connection with the extension of double-track between Roanoke and Norfolk, Va.

HISTORICAL

The line here crosses the Appomattox River and Valley, 145 miles west of Norfolk, Va., and the first bridge was built in the year 1853 as a part of the South Side R.R., connecting Petersburg and Lynchburg, Va. Information obtained from the files of the Engineering Department shows that the road was located after a careful study of the intervening country by C. O. Sanford, Chief Engineer, and built under his direction to secure not only a low first cost but an economical operation.

Briefly described, this line, after rising out of the James River Valley at Lynchburg, follows the top of the ridge which divides the waters of the Appomattox and Roanoke Rivers, in an easterly direction to

*Bridge Engineer, Norfolk & Western Ry. Co., Roanoke, Va.

Petersburg. On this location, grades of 16 ft. per mile could easily be obtained. The one exception to this is near Farmville, where it left the ridge route and crosses high above the Appomattox River Valley, returning again to the summit of the ridge several miles to the eastward.

The Chief Engineer's report shows that several conditions influenced the adoption of this route. Chief among them may be mentioned:

(1) The loss of a large amount of tonnage from Farmville if the ridge route had been followed.

(2) The residents of Farmville made an urgent appeal for the line to pass through their town, and raised a subscription to purchase stock amounting to $100,000. This, in the early stages of railroad development, was a matter of considerable moment.

(3) The adoption of the Farmville route would advance the completion of the road one year.

(4) This route was 5 miles shorter than the ridge route.

The greatest obstacle to the construction of this line was the expensive bridge over the Appomattox River and Valley.

FIRST BRIDGE — The bridge as originally built was 3100 ft. long, varying in height from 60 ft. at the abutments to 100 ft. at the river; clear spans 105 ft. in length. Previous to this time longer bridges, not so high, and higher bridges, not so long, had been built, but taking the length and height together this was thought to be the largest bridge in the world.

From a standpoint of economy, wood instead of iron was chosen for the superstructure, and was also given consideration for the piers. After an examination of a number of higher structures built of brick in several cities of the United States, and having greater unit pressures at the bottom, the successful results obtained warranted the selection of this type of construction for the piers. This decision too was influenced somewhat by the presence in the immediate vicinity of the bridge of a brick clay of superior quality, which would make the estimated cost of the piers about one-third that of stone construction.

The abutments were built of rubble masonry, and the bases of the piers to a point 3 ft. above the high-water mark were built of stone masonry with cut beds and joints. The foundations extended about 8 ft. below the ground, resting on clay and gravel. The piers were of brick masonry 8x22 ft. at the top; 14x27 ft. at the bottom and were 82 ft. high above ground. The foundations of those adjacent to the river probably extend to solid rock.

Wood superstructure was anchored to the foundation by iron rods passing entirely through the piers in shafts left for the purpose. The estimated cost of the wooden trusses of the superstructure was $18 per lin.ft., and the total cost of the bridge was $167,500. It was built to carry engines weighing 32 tons, although the ones in use at that time weighed only 16 tons.

SECOND BRIDGE — The superstructure was rebuilt in 1870 as a metal structure, the length being reduced to 21 spans, 110 ft. ¾ in. c. to c. of end bearings. It consisted of deck Fink trusses, built by the firm of Smith, Latrobe & Co., of Baltimore, of Phoenix Iron Co.'s material. The bridge was designed for a live-load of about 1850 lb. per lin.ft. of track; the spans weighed about 70,000 lb. each and were in service until 1886.

THIRD BRIDGE — In February, 1886, proposals were invited to strengthen the Fink trusses or construct a new bridge capable of sustaining loads that agree with Cooper's E-24 class, followed by a uniform load of 3000 lb. per ft., the present trusses having only 50% of the strength to safely carry this weight.

Deck Pratt trusses, built of iron, with steel eye-bars, were adopted and were fabricated and erected during the summer of 1886, the contractors being the Edge Moor Iron Co. & Frederick H. Smith. These spans were 12 ft. 2½ in. c. to c. of trusses; 15 ft. 9 in. c. to c. of chords, and consisted of seven panels 15 ft. 9 in. each, making a total length of 110 ft. 3 in. c. to c. of bearings. The ties rested directly on the top chord. The weight of metal per span was about 60,000 lb., and the bridge cost $75,000 erected in place. The record of erecting shows that five of these spans were erected under traffic in 12 days.

FOURTH BRIDGE — The 1886 spans, resting on the brick piers, carried the increased traffic until 1901, when they were reinforced by the addition of a third truss placed midway between the existing ones and braced to them. A metal floor system was added at the same time, the floor-beams resting on top of the three trusses, the middle truss being designed to carry 48% of the live load from a concentration of four 45,000-lb. axles, 5 ft. c. to c., with a uniform load of 4000 lb. per lin.ft. of track at a 10-ft. interval in either direction. These spans were built by the American Bridge Co.'s Edge Moor plant, the material being soft steel, except the eye-bars, which were of medium steel.

FIG. 1. PLACING A COMPLETELY RIVETED 72-FT. PLATE-GIRDER SPAN ON THE FARMVILLE HIGH BRIDGE, N. & W. RY.

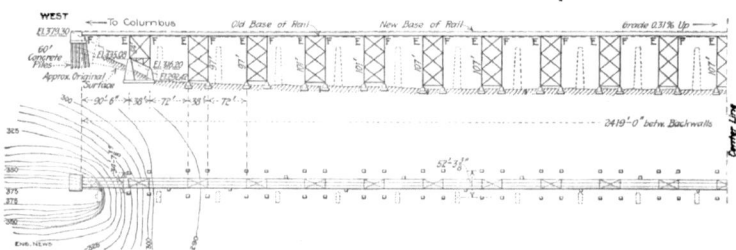

FIG. 2. PLAN AND ELEVATION OF THE NEW FARMVILLE

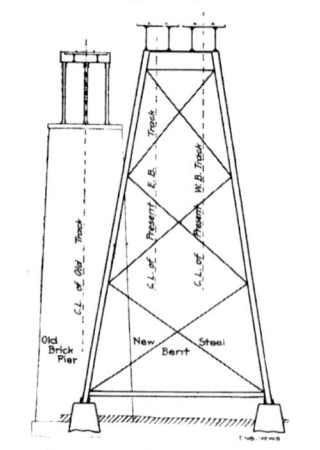

FIG. 3. COMPARATIVE CROSS-SECTIONS OF OLD AND NEW BRIDGES

This article on the building of the new High Bridge appeared in the September 10, 1914, issue of Engineering News.

The installation of the third truss and floor system was made under traffic, the grade being raised about 2 ft. to accommodate the new floor system. This latter structure carries safely the present-day traffic, with axle loads as high as 57,000 lb.

PRESENT BRIDGE

As stated above, the brick piers supporting these spans have shafts in them tapering in size from top to bottom. This condition, together with the vibration from heavy traffic, caused several of the piers to crack near the top. A number of years ago the piers were strengthened by placing bands of steel bars, at about 8-ft. intervals from the top, around the piers, connecting to angles running down the corners. These bands are clearly shown in the views.

Increased traffic which required the extension of the double-track lines into this territory, together with the appearance of additional cracks in the piers from time to time, caused a study to be made of plans for renewing this bridge for a double-track structure. Surveys were made and plans prepared in the latter part of 1912 for the construction of a double-track steel viaduct, with the center line of the near track parallel to and 20 ft. to the north of the center line of the existing bridge. The cross-section, Fig. 3, shows the relation between the old and the new structure, it being such as to permit the construction of the foundations and the erection of the steel-work without endangering the old substructure, superstructure, or interfering with traffic. Curves, near each end of the bridge, permitted the alignment to be easily adjusted on account of the offset.

Revision in the grades in this territory made it necessary to raise elevation of the base of rail on the new structure about 7 ft. higher than the old, in order to keep within the ruling grade of 0.3 against the eastbound coal traffic.

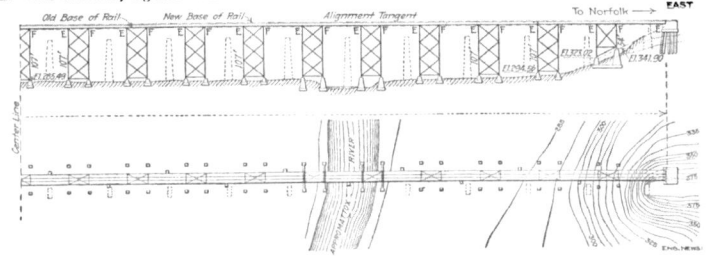

HIGH BRIDGE AND (DOTTED) THE OLD SUBSTRUCTURE

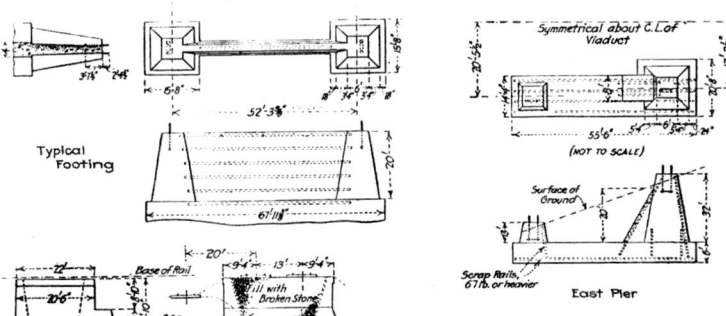

FIG. 4. DETAILS OF SUBSTRUCTURE OF FARMVILLE HIGH BRIDGE, NORFOLK & WESTERN RY.

The approach embankments at the two ends were made from borrow pits, with short haul, the material being excavated with steam shovel and dumped from light trestles alongside the fill. The materials available for making the fills contained minerals of soapstone and talc formation, which give it a disposition to slip, slides having previously occurred several times in the old embankment from this same cause. This matter was given careful consideration in the preparation of plans for the new structure, with the result that slopes of two horizontal to one vertical were adopted for the fills. As a further precaution the fill was made in three lifts, the material being placed in the outer edges of all slopes with scrapers after dumping from cars and kept in horizontal layers. A ditch was cut about 25 ft. from the foot of the slopes to care for drainage at the base. The approach fill at the west end is about 1800 ft. long; at the east end about 400 ft. long; the two contain 471,000 cu.yd.

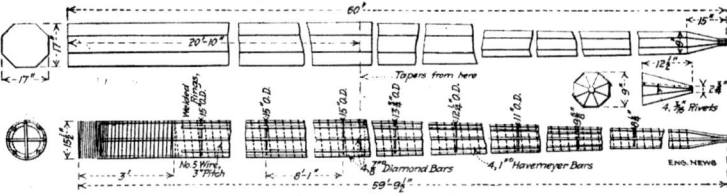

FIG. 5. DETAILS OF CONCRETE PILE

SUBSTRUCTURE—In the new structure there are 43 spans; the end or abutment spans are 90 ft. long; the intermediate spans 72 ft. long, and the tower spans 38 ft. long. The pedestals supporting the towers are 6 ft. square on top, 8 ft. 8 in. square at the base and 8 ft. high, resting on foundation courses 12 ft. 8 in. square. Foundations of this size rest on rock and give maximum load of 7.3 tons per sq.ft. The pedestals adjacent to the river were tied together with concrete struts, reinforced with steel rails, to prevent the accumulation of drift between them.

The pedestals supporting the first tower on either end vary from 20 to 40 ft. high, and the two on either side of the viaduct have a continuous foundation parallel with the track, the upper or higher pedestal is also buttressed with concrete, reinforced with steel rails, to resist the earth pressure from the fill which spills around it. The plan on Fig. 3 shows the arrangement clearly. The foundations adjacent to the river, and practically all others in the low ground, extend to rock, a distance of about 25 ft. below ground.

The abutments, U-shaped, rest on the old fill about 22 ft. below the base of rail. Broken stone fills the space between the wing walls and earth spills around the sides. Steel-rail reinforcement was liberally used in the main and wing walls of the abutments to overcome the tendency to crack from any slight settlement that may occur from shrinkage of the fill.

PILES—Reinforced-concrete piles, cast at the bridge site, were adopted to support the two abutments. Lengths of 40 to 60 ft. were required to make them penetrate to the original ground line. The outside piles were driven on a batter.

The Cummings type reinforced-concrete piles was selected and manufactured at the site and driven by the Cummings Structural Concrete Co., of Pittsburgh, Penn. They are octagonal in section; 17 in. between parallel sides for 20 ft., tapering to 9-in. section, 15 in. from the point; their design is shown in Fig. 5. Heavy spiral reinforcement, $\frac{3}{4}$-in. round; $\frac{3}{4}$- to $1\frac{1}{2}$-in. pitch, is used near the top to resist the blow of the hammer. The piles were molded during the summer and fall of 1913 on platforms underneath the forms and blocked away from the boards so that concrete would properly cover the metal. The top board was left off for pouring the concrete.

The mixture was 1:2:4, with one additional bag of cement per cubic yard of concrete, or about 1.75 bbl. of cement per cubic yard. Broken limestone, size 1 in., was used. Forms were removed after two days and piles were then allowed to cure from 30 to 60 days before driving.

A heavy frame piledriver of the ordinary type, having a drop hammer weighing 12,000 lb., was used to drive the piles. A cap, sliding between the leads, covered the top of the pile and held it in line; the blow struck was from 5 to 6 ft. fall. The piles drove hard their entire length, an average of less than two 60-ft. piles being made per day. The penetration was about $\frac{3}{4}$ in. per blow, the last foot requiring 30 to 35 blows. On this basis the piles have a resistance of 40 tons as calculated by the ENGINEERING NEWS formula, the actual load being 26 tons, including the weight of the pile, which is 6 tons; pressure per square foot on foundation bed, 1.6 tons. Good results were obtained in driving, only a small number being damaged at the top. These were cut off 3 to 4 ft. from the end.

The concrete for the pedestals and abutments was made according to Norfolk & Western standard specifications of 1:2:4 mix, with broken limestone to pass through a 2-in. ring, all dirt and dust being screened out. Good sand was secured by pumping from the river.

PLANT—The contractor's plant was located on the low ground near the west end of the bridge. All material was delivered to this plant by a low-grade track leaving the main line about one mile west. The contractor's equipment consisted of a 10-ton locomotive crane, with orange-peel bucket, used for excavating foundations. This crane also handled the concrete buckets when depositing into forms, the pile hammer to drive sheet piling and many other kinds of work in connection with this contract. Cars were used for hauling the concrete from the mixer to the various pedestals, a construction track having been laid between the pedestals from one end of the work to the other. Concrete mixers, derricks, hoisting engines were supplied to meet the requirements of handling the materials rapidly when needed. Work on the foundations and fills began in May, 1913, and was completed in April, 1914, a total of 10,908 cu.yd. of concrete being placed.

SUPERSTRUCTURE—The viaduct was designed according to the Norfolk & Western specifications of 1911 for a live-load of five 55,000-lb. axles, 5 ft. c. to c., and a uniform load of 5500 lb. per foot on either end at 10-ft. intervals. Double-web cross-girders, 7 ft. deep, were used at the top between the columns to furnish support for the two center girders, the outside girders resting directly on the column cap, diaphragms and stiffeners being used under the bearings of the center girders. The deck girders, spaced 6 ft. 6 in. c. to c., are 7 ft. 6½ in. deep, back to back of flange angles. A standard floor of 8x10-in. bridge ties 12 ft. long, dapped to 9½ in. and spaced 13 in. c. to c., is used, with 6x8-in. guard timbers outside the rails, notched down 1 in. over the ties, and 85-lb. steel guard rails inside.

The columns are made up of one cover-plate 28x$\frac{9}{16}$ in.; four angles 6x4x$\frac{7}{8}$ in., two webs 24x$\frac{7}{16}$ in., double laced on the inside, with 3x$\frac{3}{8}$-in. lace bars. Columns are built in two sections, with a batter of 2 in. in 12 in.; the base plates are 4 ft. 2 in.x5 ft.x1½ in. thick, and are anchored to the pedestals by two 1¼-in. bolts 6 ft. long, built 3 ft. 6 in. in the concrete with an anchor plate 6 in. wide, placed on the lower ends of the bolts.

The longitudinal and transverse bracing is a double system, capable of taking both tension and compression, and is made up of four angles 5x3½x$\frac{3}{8}$ in. and 6x4x$\frac{3}{8}$ in., with single lacing 2½x$\frac{3}{8}$ in. for transverse bracing, and double lacing the same dimensions for the longitudinal bracing. The bottom struts are made of two 15-in., 33-lb. channels, double laced. Tower bracing in a horizontal plane is made of four angles 5x3½x$\frac{3}{8}$ in., double laced.

ERECTION—The girders, with the exception of the two 90-ft. spans, were delivered completely riveted in pairs, and unloaded on the east end at grade alongside construction tracks. All the column sections, bracing and cross-girders were delivered and unloaded alongside the construction track running between the pedestals on the low ground.

The bottom section of each bent was erected and all bracing placed, using a 50-ton locomotive crane working on the low track. The top section of each bent was assembled and left standing alongside the bottom section, where it could be lifted to its final position with a 50-ton derrick car, using an 80-ft. boom, and working from the completed viaduct above. The top section of the near bent of each tower was placed, the derrick car standing at the end of the track over the preceding tower. The 72-ft. girder span, weighing 36½ tons, was next run out on a truck to the end of the track, and set off on the ties in a diagonal position; the derrick car next backed off the bridge so the truck could be gotten out of the way, when it returned and placed the span in position. The tower was then completed and the tower span placed.

Erection of the steel began, Apr. 1, 1914; the first span was placed, Apr. 3; last span placed, June 3; riveting completed June 11; floor laid, June 18, and traffic diverted over the new structure, June 22.

As the double track has not reached the immediate vicinity of this bridge, girders for only one track are provided at this time. The total weight of metal is 6,995,628 lb. Metal in the 99-ft. towers, per foot of height, weighed 2325 lb.; per foot of track it weighed 2000 lb. Girders, per foot of track, weighed 900 lb.; total weight of bridge as constructed, 2900 lb. per lin.ft. of track.

ENGINEERS AND CONTRACTORS

The work was started under the direction of Chas. S. Churchill, Chief Engineer; Chas. C. Wentworth, Principal Asst. Engineer, and J. E. Crawford, who, as Bridge Engineer, prepared masonry plans and supervised the design of the steelwork. It was completed under the direction of J. E. Crawford, as Chief Engineer. A. Bruner, Assistant Engineer, was in charge of all double-track construction and W. W. Vail was Resident Engineer on the work.

The Virginia Bridge & Iron Co., of Roanoke, Va., designed the steelwork, furnished and erected the structure.

Messrs. W. W. Boxley & Co., contractors, of Roanoke, Va., built the masonry and approaches.

A Fireless Locomotive for use at powder magazines and explosives storehouses has been supplied to the British navy department. It resembles a small four-wheel locomotive without a smokestack, the cylindrical tank containing some water and being charged with steam at high pressure. The steam passes through a reducing valve before reaching the valves and cylinders which are placed at the rear end of the engine. One charge is sufficient for several hours' work at steady hauling and for a still longer time in switching service, while with a pressure as low as 15 lb. the engine can run to the charging station, which is outside the danger zone. To further reduce the chance of danger from sparks the brakeshoes, bumpers, etc., are fitted with special facings. The engine was built by Andrew Barclay, Sons & Co., of Kilmarnock, Scotland.

FIG. 6. SLINGING A 60-FT. PILE ONTO THE DRIVER
FIG. 7. THE PILES IN PLACE
FIG. 8. WEAVING THE REINFORCEMENT
FIG. 9. DRAGGING A PILE FROM THE YARD UP TO THE DRIVER
FIGS. 6-9. DRIVING CONCRETE PILES ON FARMVILLE BRIDGE ACROSS APPOMATTOX VALLEY

FIG. 10. ERECTING THE NEW FARMVILLE BRIDGE OF THE NORFOLK & WESTERN RY., ACROSS THE APPOMATTOX VALLEY

HIGH BRIDGE: "THE END OF OUR FIFTEEN MONTHS' LABOR" 93

From Willis Vail's journal, June 22, 1914:

[The track forces got the east end siding cut] and moved over and connected with the new siding this morning, so that the shifter went across the bridge and distributed some ballast. I rode in the train, being the first train across the bridge. After No. 3 passed, the main line at the west end was cut and thrown over and connected to the bridge track and about 2.15 the Lynchburg, Crewe local passed over, with a through freight with Mallet engine following a little later. No. 4 was the first passenger train. Muir and Jamison jumped on it at west end and rode across. **Thus we see the end of our 15 months' labor here.**

This is an example of an annotated negative sleeve. On most sleeves, Vail recorded the negative number, the time of day, the weather conditions, camera exposure data, and the developer chemicals he used, along with a brief description of the content. This sleeve held the negative of the photo on page 35.

HIGH BRIDGE TODAY

High Bridge Trail State Park was created in 2006 when the Norfolk Southern Corporation gave thirty-one miles of abandoned railroad right-of-way to the Commonwealth of Virginia. The line originated in the 1850s as the South Side Rail Road, which connected Lynchburg and Petersburg and served as an important supply line during the American Civil War.

After receiving the property, Virginia's Department of Conservation and Recreation converted it to a multi-use trail for pedestrians, bicyclists, and equestrians. High Bridge Trail State Park officially opened to the public in 2008, and rehabilitation work on High Bridge itself was completed in 2012. Today, High Bridge is the longest pedestrian bridge in Virginia and among the longest in the nation.

High Bridge Trail State Park is popular with hikers, riders, and bicyclists. Where the trail passes through a spacious plaza in downtown Farmville, a reproduction of the 1854 South Side Rail Road freight station offers restrooms and trail information.

High Bridge forms the centerpiece of a 31-mile-long state park. The 1914 bridge has been made safe for pedestrians and other trail traffic. Three overlooks let visitors enjoy wide views of the Appomattox River valley. Piers of the 1853 bridge can be seen in the foreground.